AMERICA'S HOME TOWN
Laurel
MISSISSIPPI

"The City Beautiful"

PHOTOS BY CHAD EDWARDS
WORDS BY JIM CEGIELSKI
BOOK DESIGN BY KASSIE ROWELL

AMERICA'S HOME TOWN
LAUREL, MISSISSIPPI

Copyright © 2021, 2022 by Gin Creek Publishing Company.

Gin Creek Publishing Company,
The Laurel Leader-Call and the Gin Creek logo
are trademarks or registered trademarks
owned by Gin Creek Publishing Company.

All rights reserved. No part of this publication
may be reproduced, copied, stored, or transmitted in any form
or by any means, electronic, mechanical, photocopying,
recording, or otherwise, without written permission
of Gin Creek Publishing Company.

ISBN: 978-0-578-30674-2
Printed in the USA

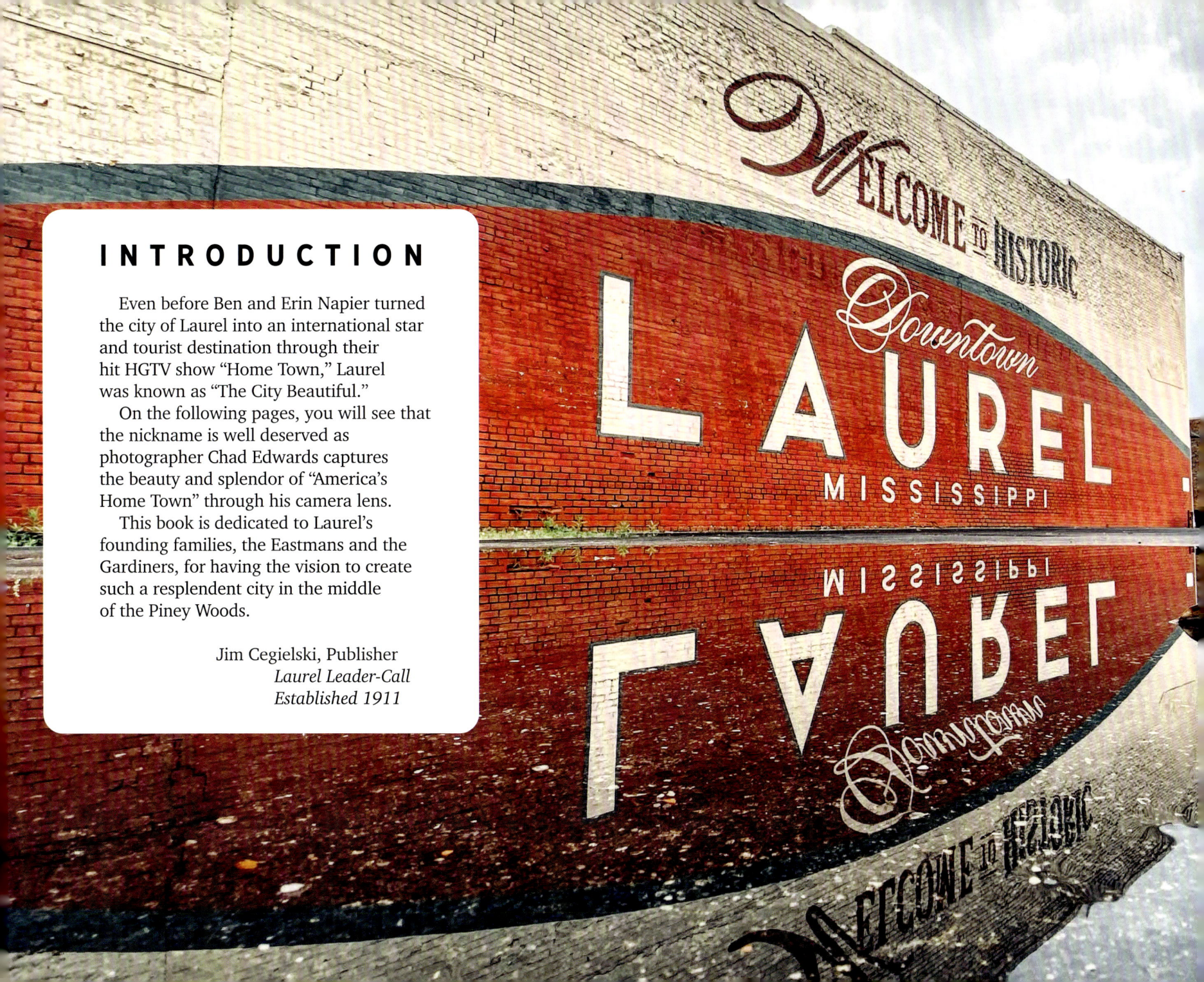

INTRODUCTION

Even before Ben and Erin Napier turned the city of Laurel into an international star and tourist destination through their hit HGTV show "Home Town," Laurel was known as "The City Beautiful."

On the following pages, you will see that the nickname is well deserved as photographer Chad Edwards captures the beauty and splendor of "America's Home Town" through his camera lens.

This book is dedicated to Laurel's founding families, the Eastmans and the Gardiners, for having the vision to create such a resplendent city in the middle of the Piney Woods.

Jim Cegielski, Publisher
Laurel Leader-Call
Established 1911

"LIVE IN LAUREL" CONCERT

DOWNTOWN "HOME TOWN" SHOWING

FIFTH AVENUE AND CENTRAL AVENUE

NORTH MAGNOLIA STREET

NORTH MAGNOLIA STREET

NORTH MAGNOLIA STREET

THE COURTYARD AT 320 FIFTH STREET

320 FIFTH STREET

CAFÉ LA FLEUR

PEARL'S DINER

FLAG POLE ROUNDABOUT

TRAIN DEPOT

NORTH MAGNOLIA STREET

THE ARABIAN

LAUREL LITTLE THEATRE

PINEHURST PARK

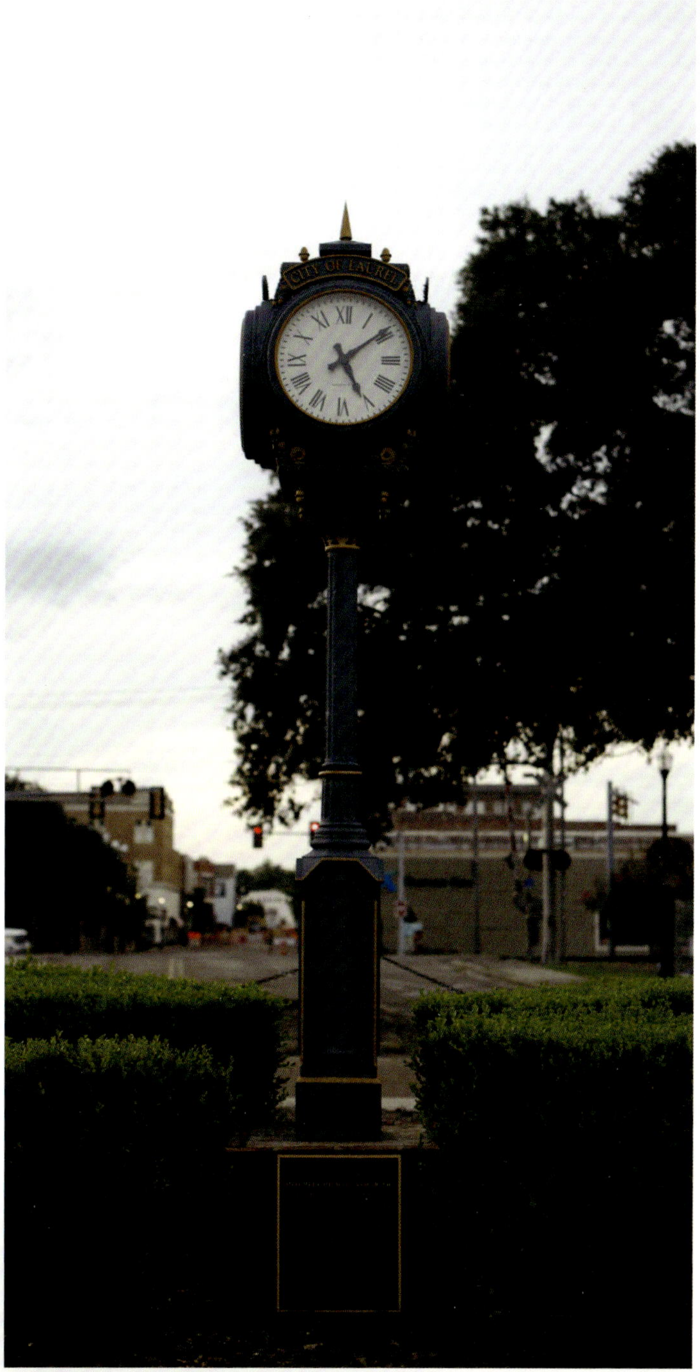
CITY OF LAUREL
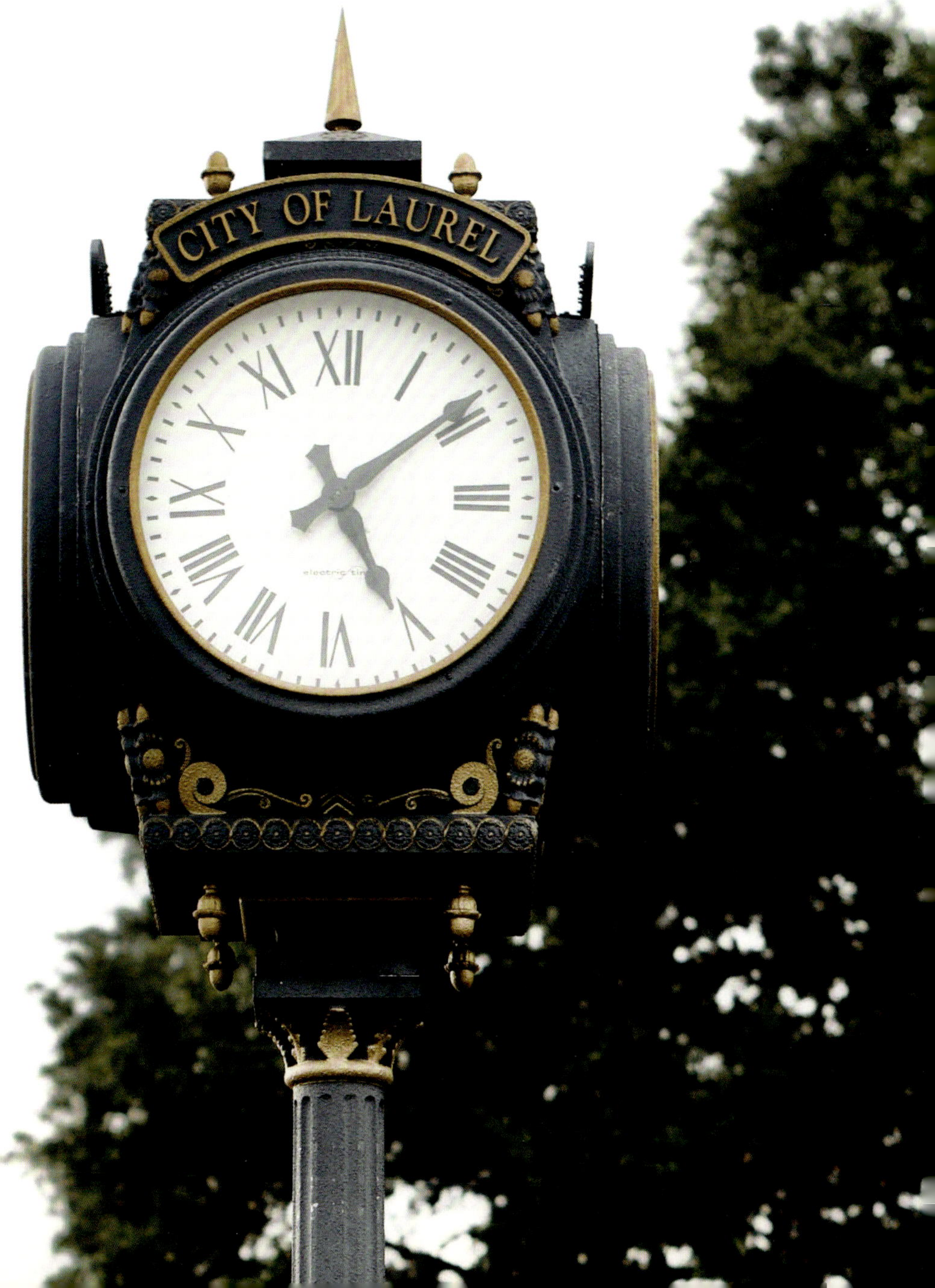
CITY OF LAUREL

OUTDOOR ART GALLERY IN LEONTYNE PRICE PARK

EVERYTHING IS GONNA BE *okay*

Laurel LOOKS GOOD ON YOU

LAUREN ROGERS MUSEUM OF ART

FIFTH AVENUE

WISTERIA BED AND BREAKFAST

FIFTH AVENUE

ROGERS-GREEN HOUSE

HISTORIC HOME

THE GREEN HOME

HISTORIC HOME

FIFTH AVENUE

ROGERS-GREEN HOUSE

HISTORIC HOME

OAK STREET

EASTMAN, GARDINER & COMPANY BUILDING

CENTRAL AVENUE

PINEHURST PARK

CORNER OF OAK & NORTH MAGNOLIA

ST. JOHN'S EPISCOPAL CHURCH

FIRST TRINITY PRESBYTERIAN CHURCH

FIRST BAPTIST CHURCH OF LAUREL

LAUREL FIRST UNITED METHODIST CHURCH

JONES COUNTY COURTHOUSE
LAUREL

TRUSTMARK BUILDING

CENTRAL AVENUE

FILMING ERIN NAPIER INSIDE LEE'S COFFEE & TEA

VISITORS ENJOYING THE LAUREN ROGERS MUSEUM OF ART'S WALKING TOUR OUTSIDE OF WISTERIA B&B.

LAUREL LEADER-CALL
EST. 1911